Pain and Gain: How I Survived and Triumphed

An Uplifting Story of Thriving after a Traumatic Experience

Marc Schiller

DEDICATION

To the memory of my father, mother and sister, who always put up a fight, never gave up, and instilled that spirit within me.

Contents

ACKNOWLEDGMENTS

Editing- Talia Leduc
Special thanks to Stephanie D. Schiller, Alex
(Moose) Schiller, David J. Schiller, Edward DuBois
III, and Gene Rosen.

CHAPTER 1

Life's Journey

"Each difficult moment has the potential to open my eyes and open my heart"—Myla Kabat-Zinn

Although we believe that we are born and die only once, the truth is that throughout our lives, we die and are reborn many times. As outlandish as this statement may appear, traumatic experiences are usually the trigger for these transformations, catapulting us to new facets of life that we would otherwise not experience. Many times, these experiences make us change course. That is, if we pay heed to their messages. I'm only one of countless humans on this planet who can tell such a story as this, but I beg everyone to share in this message. My experience was extreme in the sense that I faced almost certain death. Regardless, those with less extreme experiences can still relate to the message of this book, which remains relevant even though our own events vary in degree. Facing adversity and emerging victorious is truly a triumph of the body, mind and spirit. We are all capable of not only overcoming these events but also learning their lessons and charting new courses in our lives, resulting in our growth and enrichment as individuals.

The birth of this book was a natural byproduct of my previous book, in which I narrated an unbelievable but true story. That book, *Pain and Gain: The Untold True Story*, was the final chapter is my cleansing process. It was also a detailed account of an event that changed the course of my life and who I was. There are certain events that we either use to turn ourselves in a new direction or that leave us in a state of stagnation, unable to move forward. These events can, in many cases, leave us in a comatose state, searching for answers as to why these things happened to us. In fact, the answer is simply that since we did not heed prior warnings, the universe has shaken us into listening. That choice is always up to us. We consciously decide how these sometimes bitter and harsh lessons will help us to find answers and move forward or cower and give up all hope. It must be said that in these most difficult moments in our lives, finding strength and courage is not easy, but these qualities do lie within each one of us. We may just not be aware of them.

I have often been asked if I had done something different that day or not gone about my normal daily routine, then, perhaps, I would not have gone through what I did and could have completely avoided those events. I do not believe so. Life is a simple game of probabilities, and, for some unknown reason, those events had to occur. If I had avoided that event, another event, perhaps even worse, would have occurred later on. There was a reason for what happened to me, a wake-up call, perhaps. There was no evading it, even though I might foolishly believe that if I had done something different then, I could have. Speculating on what could or could not have happened is a foolhardy exercise and does not lead to any benefits or any answers or growth. Events happen, and the important thing is how we respond to them. I do not ask why these things happened to me. Instead, I ask how this tragic event can transform me and help me grow into a better human being.

Now, from this perspective, I'm able to see more clearly the process that I went through to overcome and move forward from those events in 1994 and afterwards. It was not an easy road, and it was filled with obstacles and hills to climb. The easiest course of action would have been to quit and curl into a ball in some corner, simply looking for the pity and sympathy of others as a crutch, all the while trying to deny what had really occurred and shelter my mind from the memories of it. This approach would have provided no benefit, nor would it have opened new doorways to better myself and learn important life lessons. It would have left too many unresolved issues and may have mentally handicapped me for the rest of my life.

Is the process simple? No, but you have to make a choice: Let the experience consume you, or try to reap all the lessons it offers you. Does this require courage? Yes, because you have to have the mental tenacity to pull yourself together again. Does everyone possess the courage and mental tenacity to overcome any situation? Yes, absolutely. They just have to make a conscious decision that this is their intent, their direction, and the road they will take, and be prepared for whatever they find along the way.

You often hear of individuals who have gone through life-changing events and emerged victorious while, for others, life takes a never-ending downward spiral because of their refusal to deal with the issues head on. The difference is simply that the victorious ones saw their events as an opportunity, not a defeat.

Indulging in self-pity or seeking the pity of others can paralyze us, not allowing us to move forward. One must always be on guard not to fall into a trap, which is extremely difficult to escape from. These tendencies may be comforting, perhaps, in the short run, but they are lethal in the long run.

For me, the recovery process involved healing my body, mind and spirit. Although these elements are intertwined, each uniquely offered its own set of challenges and opportunities for growth. I want to share with you how I went through this process after nearly losing my life. It was not easy, but I'm much richer both spiritually and mentally now as a result of it. I have learned and grown. By sharing my experience, I hope that some can relate to and benefit from my words.

CHAPTER 2

The Events

"I assess the power of a will by how much resistance, pain, torture it endures and knows how to turn to its advantage"—Friedrich Nietzsche

The events that forever changed my life and who I am started on November 15, 1994. Up to that point, I led what could have been considered a pretty normal life, with its ups and downs, but nothing dramatic one way or the other. My life was made up of routine and the occasional challenge. I was not a religious or spiritual person and paid too little attention to that aspect of my life. I was totally immersed in making money and in my family, particularly my young children. That day, November 15, 1994, the way I saw the world and myself was turned upside down. Nothing, and I mean nothing, was ever going to be the same. I could never have foreseen the events that were to unfold, but you would have to have a very wild imagination to do so. Even then, you might tell yourself that things like that just don't happen in this great country.

Prior to that day in November, I had run an accounting business from my home, and I owned a deli that was located near Miami Airport. The deli required my attendance every day for about six hours because it was the type of business where your employees would rob you blind if you weren't there. This was the only time I really ventured out of the house, except for family outings and to run errands. I was the epitome of a homebody. The time I was not working I spent with my wife and two young children. I did not socialize, nor did I have friends. Life revolved around work, family, and home. In fact, I had closed my accounting office and begun doing the work from home so that I did not have to spend all day there. Most clients either brought the work to my house or a former employee of mine would pick it up and bring it to me.

We were a comfortable middle-class family living in a middle-class neighborhood. We had nothing ostentatious or anything that would make us stand out. Our neighbors would have a hard time recalling us if you asked them since we kept to ourselves. We were the model family living the model American life.

Life was not always that simple or good. I was born in Argentina and as a young child had to go through many hardships. We lived in the countryside in abject poverty. We did not even possess such basic necessities as electric service, running water and most of the time food. The school I went to consisted of one room with a dirt floor. During our last year there my father immigrated to the United States to seek a better life. This left my mother, older sister, baby brother and I to fend for ourselves in a very difficult environment.

Once we arrived in the United States we moved to one of the worst neighborhoods in Brooklyn. The best way I can describe it was that it was a war zone. Although my father made enough money to feed us and give us a roof over our heads, everything else was up to me. So by the time I was eight I was already an entrepreneur selling refundable bottles, carrying groceries home for shoppers, delivering TV guides or doing anything else I could think of to earn a dime, a quarter, or if I was very lucky a dollar. Through high school and college I worked to pay for both school and subsistence. Although the scenario I described may seem harsh to many. It gave the mental tenacity and strength to deal with and overcome any situation that at first appeared as a formidable challenge. It was precisely the way I grew up that built the character that would help me survive my kidnapping. It was as if my whole life had been training for that particular event.

November 15, 1994 the day of my kidnapping started out normally, but never did I imagine, that morning when I left my house for work, that I would never return to the place I had called home for the previous four years. My world and that of my family was totally turned upside down. Nothing would ever be the same. I describe in full detail what occurred for the next thirty days in my previous book. However, I will give a brief synopsis of the events so you can understand the obstacles I faced during and after the period of my stay in what I termed "Hotel Hell."

I was a creature of habit and was always home by a certain time. That day, I stayed longer at the deli, waiting for a prospective buyer who never did keep his appointment. As I left the deli and walked outside, I was approached and forcefully grabbed by three unknown men. I first thought it was a simple mugging or that they wanted to steal my car, but I was beaten, Tasered, and eventually dragged to a waiting van. This was not a simple robbery, as I had first surmised.

After being tossed into the van, I thought this was some type of hit and that I was going to be taken somewhere and killed. Both guesses were wrong, and I did not have a clue at the time that my kidnapping would begin an ordeal of torture, humiliation, starvation and darkness that would last for thirty days. Upon being thrown into the van, my eyes were duct taped, and I was handcuffed, both hands and feet. I entered a world of darkness where my freedom and self-determination had been lost. That was my welcome to Hotel Hell.

During my captivity, I was not only subjected to subhuman conditions and treatment but was routinely tortured. The torture involved beatings, Taserings, Russian roulette, the burning of my limbs, and other assorted cruelties that brought joy and laughter to my captors but pain and misery to me. My captors tried to torture me not only physically but also mentally. Fortunately, I was well equipped and prepared for that.

From the onset, my only immediate concern was the safety of my wife and children. Once I knew they were safely out of harm's way, the ordeal became a mental match that consisted of my captors dishing out their cruel torture and seeing how much I could withstand. I never buckled, gave in, or lost my spirit to survive. I always believed that somehow, I was going to survive that episode and that I would one day be free from the chains that bound me.

I was always blindfolded, and balls of wax were stuck in my ears. I spent most of my days in a box chained to a wall. Other days, I was chained in a bathroom, where the heat soared, with no water to drink. Later on in my captivity, they would throw me in the trunk of my car. I was hardly fed and lost thirty-seven pounds during that month. I was used as a cruel joke to satisfy their deranged enjoyment. Still, I never faltered and held my spirits high.

They financially raped me of everything I

owned. They cleaned my bank accounts, used my credit cards, and took my home. They moved into my house, living what was supposed to be my life, sleeping in my bed and eating my food. All the while, I starved, bled and rotted, chained to a wall in that warehouse. Still I never lost hope.

I was treated like an animal on a leash, with a cruel master. Still my faith never wavered. They withheld food and gave me no water to drink. Still I held my head up high.

They humiliated me by not allowing me to use the bathroom facilities, so I had to urinate on myself or use cups. They bounced me off walls and played other cruel games to satisfy their sick minds. Still I held steadfast and did not submit. They could do many things to me, but they could not break my spirit or my will to survive.

My captors were infuriated that they had done everything they could to break me without success and they hoped that I would break down in tears and beg for mercy. They made one mistake:

They did not know or understand me. That was not going to happen. That was one miscalculation they had made.

They got tired of their games, and seeing that there was nothing left to take from me, they decided to dispose of me. Their plan was to murder me, but they were going to make it look like an accident and collect my life insurance. The story they concocted was that I was having a midlife crisis, which included a new girlfriend, and the passion had driven me to drink and kill myself in an accident. This story was so ludicrous and outlandish that I thought no one would ever believe it, but it almost worked.

The evening of December 14, 1994 after thirty days of withstanding every cruelty imaginable, I was convinced that I was going to die. I did not beg for them to spare my life, nor did I fall into a state of depression or despair. I accepted my fate serenely and reached a state of peace and acceptance, knowing that I had been able to save my family. I may have been humiliated, but I never lost my dignity. Even at that point, I did not lose hope. I would not—there was always a slim chance of those things we call miracles.

They drugged me, and, while I was unconscious, they drove my car to a desolate place and crashed it into a utility pole to mimic an accident. Then they poured gasoline on the car and me and set it on fire. I do not recall how, since I was supposedly unconscious, but I managed to get out of the car. They were shocked and proceeded to run me over twice with their vehicle. I was surely dead, they must have surmised. Wrong. I survived. They forgot about one thing: *miracles*.

Someone was looking after me that evening in December and knew that my mission in this life was not over, that I had more to do, either for the good of another or myself. It was simply not time for me to make my exit.

CHAPTER 3

Mental State of Captivity

"A man who is 'of sound mind' is one who keeps the inner madman under lock and key."—Paul Valery

When I think of the days I spent in the warehouse, it reminds me of a quote by Mahatma Gandhi: "You can chain me, you can torture me, you can even destroy this body, but you will never imprison my mind."

I will not pretend that I was always optimistic and cheery during my captivity. But, during my ordeal, I was keenly aware that keeping my mind sharp and spirit in tact were the keys to my survival. My captivity was an emotional rollercoaster ride that, at times, forced me to use every ounce of my strength to stay focused and to keep reminding myself that my survival depended on my inner strength, my metal tenacity.

I can break down my captivity into two phases. The first lasted about four days, during which I did not know what was happening. It was this uncertainty that caused me anxiety, the greatest angst due to my inability to control my family's safety. This was the one variable that kept me in a state of mental commotion. My first and only priority was to get them to safety.

My kidnapers threaten to bring my wife and children to the warehouse. They told me that they would take turns raping my wife as I watched. They also told me that they would chain my son who was six and daughter who was two next to me. I did not believe that these were idle threats. These were desperate individuals that I believed would do desperate things to get what they were after, money. So I made a proposal. That I would cooperate and give them everything if in return they would let my wife and children leave the country and go to Colombia. They accepted my terms and two days later my family flew out of the country and out of harm's way.

Once I was able to secure my family's safety and they were out of harm's way, a huge burden was lifted from my shoulders and the game and my demeanor changed. I had accomplished my mission, and now my survival depended on some variables I better could control. It became a test to see how mentally strong I was and how much I could endure.

My captors had lost their leverage on me. I was now relaxed and was able to get my rationality back and focus on playing the game. I had always been a survivor, and though the game, the players and the environment were all new to me, I never went down without a fight. It was just not who I was. There were difficult times when despair tried to set in, but I always willed myself to fight. My motto became "Bring it on." I knew that in order to survive I needed to keep my mind and spirit strong, and I was dammed if they were going to take that from me.

There were times that I had to pick myself up, especially in the beginning, when the cruel reality set in that I was alone. There would be no rescue, no cavalry, and no SWAT team. I was my own, and my survival depended on me. Everything depended on my will to survive and on how well I could control my emotions. Early in my captivity, I had hit a low spot, but, like a phoenix rising from the ashes, my spirit rose. I was not going down that path. I promised myself to fight on, and if the eventuality was death, so be it. I was going out with dignity and on my own terms. I had always been a fighter, and the circumstances did not change that. I told myself that self-pity was not warranted and could only undermine my struggle to survive.

Were there moments when I wanted to just throw in the towel? Sure, perhaps more than one. Each day, there were lunacies and surprises from my captors. Each day was a challenge. Each day required digging deep down inside for the inner strength to face it, but in my heart I knew I was up to it.

I have always been in good physical condition, but as the days in the warehouse wore on and I lay or sat chained on the warehouse floor, my physical condition and body's and strength began to deteriorate. That, combined with fact that I had little or no nutrition, exacerbated the situation. There were days when simply getting up from that warehouse floor and walking was a challenge. However, I knew that more than ever, my mental state needed to compensate for my weakening body.

I felt no fear. I was at peace with myself. I always felt in control, even though the circumstances should have indicated otherwise. I felt powerful, although others would say I was in a position of weakness. Power and control lie within, not outside of oneself.

My captors were perplexed and commented that I was too calm. They said that I was taking everything so well. They did not know or understand me. As long as I could keep control of my emotions, something I have always done well, it would come down to a duel of the minds, and I felt I had the advantage. My body may have been withering, but my mind was sharp as a tack. As long as it remained that way, those boys had met their worst nightmare.

The monotony was the most difficult thing to deal with, sitting in the same position day in and day out with no external stimuli and very limited room to move. There was no day or night since I had temporarily lost my eyesight from having three rolls of duct tape secured head covering my eyes.

In this kind of situation, you have to control your thoughts or they will undermine you. Easier said than done. Your mind starts to wander and creates scenarios that play out over and over like a rerun of a movie. I asked myself, *What if this? What if that?* Knowing full well that those thoughts although entertaining. Did not serve any useful purpose and just made me anxious.

So I quieted my mind as much as possible and just stared into the void of darkness most of the time. I guess, looking back, I was in a meditational state that afforded me the peace I needed to come up with solutions.

Of course my captors tried their hardest to upset this balance. They would play loud music that was not only disquieting but also showed their bad taste. At first, it was difficult to even think with such a loud racket, and it made me feel nervous and uncomfortable. I eventually learned to tune it out. Many days, I hardly noticed or paid attention to it. I was on a mission of survival, and I was not going to be deterred.

Days seem to last weeks, hours seemed like days, and minutes felt like hours. Thirty days after setting foot in that warehouse, the day I was supposed to die arrived. I convinced that those were my last hours on this planet, and accepted this calmly and with dignity. I did not beg for mercy I did not try to dissuade the men plotting my murder. I just sat there and stared into the darkness, asking God to forgiven me for those I may have hurt in my lifetime. Most importantly, I thought about my family. They were safe, and that was what mattered. I felt that I had done all I could and did not fear what I knew was about to come. I was in total peace. So I waited. Then I was drugged, and the world swam away.

When I woke up, I was in the ICU of Jackson Memorial Hospital. As I said, I believe in miracles. To the chagrin of my captors, I had survived. I was not ready to go yet. For me, new challenges lay ahead, and I would need all my mental strength to be able to confront them. My first priority was to go after the criminals who had done this to me and make sure they wore chains of their own—forever.

CHAPTER 4

The Body

"To keep the body in good health is a duty. . . . Otherwise we shall not be able to keep our mind strong and clear"—Buddha

Waking up in the ICU of the hospital was no pleasurable experience. I had been through a six-hour operation in which I lost my spleen and had my bladder repaired. My pelvis had been shattered, and I had burns and lacerations throughout my body, especially on my butt. I had been opened like a cantaloupe and had fifty-four staples running from my chest to my pubic hair. My eyes were bloody from the tape. I had a catheter in place and tubes sticking from every possible part of my body. The first thing the nurse told me was that they feared that I might be paralyzed because my spine had been severely twisted. I never realized pain could be so acute; it was a pain that cannot be described in words. Yet, at that moment, I felt appreciation and was grateful for the blessing to be alive. I knew that my survival was miraculous.

Did I forget to mention what I looked like? Not having shaved for a month—or showered, for that matter— I was quite a sight, and the smell that my body emitted could not have been pleasant to anyone standing close by.

The first few days were difficult, as I swam in and out of consciousness. Falling asleep was my only reprieve from the intolerable pain. When I was awake, my mind was sharp, and I knew what needed to be done. I was now accompanied by my brother, Alex, and sister, Michelle, who were my allies and were there for anything I needed.

The days I spent in Jackson Memorial Hospital in Miami were not pleasant. My poor physical condition combined with the fear that those who had tortured me would return made everything more intense. By Friday of that same week, I was on my way to New York to hopefully begin healing and picking up the pieces of my shattered and now nonexistent life.

We left not a moment too soon. My tormentors and kidnappers arrived two hours after our departure to kill me and anyone else with me. That was a close call.

In the New York hospital, I began relaxing a little, and I started the slow process of healing. I was able to shave for the first time in five weeks, and the pain slowly subsided to being bearable. I was awake more often and had company, which made adjusting a little easier. I was also able to begin eating some easily digestible items, like Jell-O, before that I could not keep anything down.

On Christmas Eve 1994, the doctor came in and

told me that I could go home if I could manage to walk a few steps with crutches. I needed no further encouragement and told him, "Let's do it." I was extremely weak and almost fell while getting out of bed. Fortunately, the orderly was able to catch me. He took me down to the exercise room, where I could demonstrate my walking skills for him. The pain in trying to do so was excruciating. With grit and determination and tears in my eyes from the pain, I managed to walk a few feet with crutches, which was good enough. I was given the green light to leave the hospital. I was overwhelmed with joy, even though I knew that immense challenges lay ahead. At that moment, it did not matter. I felt victorious and knew that I would be able to face whatever was to come my way.

Before I left, I was reminded of what torture was like as the doctor removed the fifty-four staples and not so gently pulled the catheter tube from my penis. This time, it was different, and I grinned and bore the pain since I knew it meant I was one step closer to my freedom.

As I was wheeled out of the hospital that evening, it was the first time I could feel a breeze in my face and breathe open air. I was free. Tears rolled down my cheeks as I realized that I had just been reborn. The person who was dragged into that warehouse had indeed died there, and this was a new version of me who had exited those hospital doors.

It was time to heal physically before I was totally ready for the mental challenges that lay ahead. At first, it was difficult to accept that I needed help doing normal things that I had been accustomed to doing on my own, things that I would have never thought about, like walking, getting up from a bed and even being able to go to the bathroom. Since I could not move my legs, someone had to put them on the floor so I could use the crutches to prop myself up. A stool had to be put in the shower so I could sit while I went about the job of cleaning the grime I had accumulated for a month. Indeed, life had changed for me.

My sister would take me outside and sit with me. She said I was yellow and needed some color. It was January in New York, so you could imagine how cold it was. Nonetheless, the feeling of freedom was empowering, and the smells of nature were a sweet perfume.

Slowly I mastered the use of the crutches, and the pain and stiffness in my legs began to subside. It was bearable. My appetite retuned slowly, and my sister was always there to pamper me with whatever my heart desired. The first month showed marked improvement in my health, and at the end of January I went to visit the doctor. He informed me that my injuries were healing well and that I would soon be able to walk without crutches.

I was in much better physical condition at the beginning of February and decided that, for the safety of all, it would be better if I left the country. Using my crutches, I dragged myself on the plane and went to my wife's home country of Colombia.

For the next two months, my recovery was

steady, and I began to be able to bend my legs and start walking without my crutches. My appetite began to return to normal. The wounds began to heal, but the scars they left were a grotesque reminder of what I had endured. It would be a long time before they would fade.

A year later, you would have never suspected the extent of my injuries. I had for the most part fully recuperated. The only thing that gave my ordeal away was the deep scars that I would wear for the rest of my life. I felt blessed that, despite the traumas I had suffered, there were no lingering ramifications or side effects from my injuries. Another miracle had occurred

My experience taught me that our bodies reflect our mental state. I suffered severe injuries but was determined not only to overcome them but also recuperate quickly. To an outsider it would appear that I willed my body to heal rapidly because I would not have it any other way. I needed my health to face the challenges that were ahead.

CHAPTER 5

Emotions

"One ought to hold on to one's heart; for if one lets it go, one soon loses control of the head too"—
Friedrich Wilhelm Nietzsche

Emotions appear to be the biggest obstacles for humans to conquer. Although they may serve us well in certain circumstances, they can be detrimental and cause great harm in others. Knowing how to control our emotions in dire situations is not only vital but can mean the difference between life and death.

I have always been able to control my emotions and have nerves of steel. This has served me well but has also caused me problems, because people have not understood where I am coming from.

In 1993, my son nearly drowned in our pool. A family member pulled him out of the water and just stood there, looking at his lifeless body. I immediately ran to him and began giving CPR while everyone else was screaming and in a commotion. They could not control their emotions sufficiently to call 911. While I was giving him CPR, I yelled for the telephone and calmly called for rescue. My being able to control my emotions saved his life that day. The same demeanor would help save mine.

I cannot honestly say that I was totally in control of my emotions the first twenty-four hours of my ordeal. It was chaotic, and I was bewildered as to what was occurring. Under such great duress, control was not a simple task. This combined with my concern for the safety of my family made the first phase of my captivity a difficult emotional roller coaster ride.

After this short period of time, when I realized what was going on and who was involved, I was able to begin to get a grip. I needed to do so, as the hours and days that lay ahead could very well determine the fate of family's safety. This was made more difficult because the first few days were when I received the most sadistic and intense torture of my captivity. I was able to control my despair, anger, fear and a host of other emotions in order to handle what needed to be done. This was typical of who I had always been.

Over the next few days, I was anxious as I awaited my family's departure, but I hid my feelings well, and my captors were not able to discern any change in my behavior that they could use to their advantage. I imagine they were perplexed by my totally calm and business-like attitude, though I was not surprised by this ability to harness my emotions.

After my family was out of harm's way, controlling my emotions became easier. I had a poker face most of the time, which they could not see because of the tape and hood over my face. If they were looking for clues in the way I acted or in what I said, there were none to be found. I did have periods when the humiliation and cruel treatment caused me to get flustered and even angry, but I never showed it. In these circumstances, I reminded myself that being cool, calm and collected was of the utmost importance, and being emotional would only cloud my judgment, something I could not afford.

As time passed, my inactivity would cause despair and irritability. It took all the strength I could muster not to do something illogical in my anger. There was only one situation in which I did finally lose my cool. The tape around my eyes was eating into my skin, and the itching and pain had become unbearable. I lashed out and told the watchman that unless he did something about the tape around my eyes, I was going to rip it off. I told him, "You know what? Just go ahead and shoot me." It worked, and he put a sanitary napkin beneath the tape, which alleviated the pain and itching. It was the only time that I lost control. It did not have repercussions, but more outbursts like that could have.

Most of the time, I just waited and said nothing. Patience is a virtue. It was not that I lost hope and chose to become docile and obedient—I was waiting for an opportunity, any opportunity to arise, this required being in control all the time.

Once I was out of the warehouse, I was emotionally exhausted and basically felt nothing. I could not. I had been on a marathon of emotions for a month, and I was drained. I could not feel anything. Slowly but surely, I returned to normal over the next few months. However, it was difficult; as such experiences leave deep emotional scars that are slow to heal.

The reunion with my family was an emotional and tearful experience. I was certain that I would never see them again. Fortunately, my children were young and oblivious to what was really happening and that was a blessing. My son David just wanted to pick where we left and play games. He was not curious why Dad was walking on crutches and never asked what happened to me. My daughter, Stephanie or Pudgies as we affectionately called her and still do, was only two. She loved to sit on my shoulders and jump up and down. She wondered why I did not want to play our familiar game. I really could not explain to her about my injuries. My children brought a smile to my face. They made me forget the tragedy I had been through, at least for a moment. A few years ago I sat down with both of them and told them what happened. I strongly believed that they needed to know. They were shocked. For them life never really changed. There was just a pause when Dad was not home for a month.

My recovery was not yet over. With the help

of private investigator Ed DuBois, I was still trying without luck to get the police to listen to me and arrest the criminals. This was an exasperating emotionally taxing experience. No matter how much evidence we obtained, the police did not believe our story. We spent months gathering evidence, to no avail. The fact that I knew who two of the kidnappers were since I recognized the voice of one and the name of another had been openly mentioned during my captivity did not help or make our case stronger.

After I went to police in April 1995 and realized that they were not going to pursue my kidnappers, I felt another layer of emotional baggage on top of the one I already carried. This was an emotional low point, and I had to prod myself to move forward. I was depressed and angry that I could not put this episode of my life behind me. Once again, I realized that the only things I could control were within, not outside of me.

I had become a prisoner again within a

strange land. I could not leave Columbia and return home to the United States since the criminals, who surely still wanted to kill me, were running free. I decided that I would try to forget what I could not have by paying attention to the things I could control. I spent more time with my children, who not only brought me joy but also sheltered me from the storm.

The calm would not last. Less than two months after I had gone to the police, I received a call that there had been another possible kidnapping that appeared very similar to mine. They feared the young couple was dead, and they asked me if I would come to help prosecute their killers. This broke the dam of emotions that had slowly built up over the months, and I was deeply saddened. I knew we had done everything possible to avoid another tragedy. It was not to be. I had to tell and retell my story each time experiencing the entire episode once again in full-color detail.

The next three years were, to say the least,

emotionally charged. I spent countless hours with the prosecutors, trying to build a case against the Sun Gym Gang, as my captors, now murderers, had become known. It was not difficult to prove their guilt, as there was a mountain of evidence, but for me the investigation caused a whirlwind of emotions the entire time.

It all finally culminated in 1998, when I had to find the inner strength to testify in court and confront those who had tried to take my life. Testifying was not as difficult as some may think it would be, because I knew they could no longer do me any harm. This sad and tumultuous episode was finally coming to a close.

In 1996 and 1997, I had other issues to deal with that required me to put aside my own woes. On the same day that I was kidnapped, my sister, who had always been my ally and closest friend, had found out she had breast cancer. The disease progressed, but at times it seemed that she would recuperate. In 1996, things took a turn for the worse, and she went from city to city and from treatment to treatment. I was always there and accompanied her. I had to put my self-pity aside and had to be strong, not for me but for her.

There was no letup, and now I found myself trying to give her the emotional support she needed to face her challenges. It is difficult when you cannot control how someone else feels. I knew her feelings were up to her, but I nonetheless tried to be there to distract her from her illness. I think it was a special time for both of us. We forgot about our worries and laughed. We would sit down, watch movies and play backgammon for hours. At times, both our problems seemed to be distant. But that would be short lived.

In January 1997, while I was taking her to one of her chemotherapy sessions, she said to me, out of the blue, "Marc, I'm not going to die, am I?" I felt as though I had been hit with a hammer. What could I say? Obviously, I said no, but on that day I was not sure of anything anymore.

In February, her condition deteriorated further, and she decided to go to Philadelphia for an experimental treatment. I was exhausted. Having spent the past month with her, I decided to take a break and be with my family. You have to understand that my sister was a rock, an island, and a person who never showed any emotions. She broke down and cried, and she asked me to please go with her to Philadelphia. I was confused. She was going with her husband and two daughters, unlike other times during which I had taken her alone to her treatments. She persisted, and, seeing her unusual demeanor, I called my wife and told her that I had postponed my trip for two days. We went to Philadelphia, and I slept in a cot close to her.

We had arrived on a Sunday, and by Tuesday things seemed stable. I kissed her goodbye on the forehead and told her I would be back the following week. She just smiled at me. I went to the airport and boarded the plane to see my family. As I flew home, my sister passed away at the young age of forty-four. Two different tragedies had started on that same day in 1994, with two different outcomes. Now, please try to tell me we are not here for a purpose and that, until it is complete, we do not leave this planet.

When I arrived home and was told the news, I was an emotional basket case. It was easier for me to handle my own trauma than the loss of my sister and friend. I could have just thrown in the towel at that point, and perhaps some would have. However, I knew that I was strong and that my sister would have wanted me to fight on and never give up. We were cut from the same cloth, and she never gave up hope. Neither would I. After shedding my tears at her funeral, I returned home to Miami to face the final episode of my own travesty.

It seemed that life had decided to throw me some curveballs and see how much punishment I could endure. I looked at myself in the mirror and decided that I was going to move forward no matter what and that I possessed the inner mental and spiritual strength to overcome anything that life would throw at me. I have never looked back. Each day, I live to the fullest and give thanks for all the blessings I receive.

CHAPTER 6

The Mind

"*The mind is not a vessel to be filled, but a fire to be kindled*"—Plutarch

Fortunately, during my days in that warehouse, I was able to keep a clear head, and this helped me make rational decisions. I'm a logical and rational individual, by nature, always have been, and I was that way during those days. I continually looked for clues and anything that could give me an edge, seeking ways to obtain my freedom and save my life, if that was possible. At times, it became frustrating, because from the position I was in, options were limited, as was my ability to control my destiny.

It may come as a surprise to some that I never lost my sense of humor during those dark days when I was chained to that wall. I would either poke fun at the surroundings, my captors or myself. It was a way to maintain both my sanity and humanity. Of course, most of these jokes occurred in my mind. I dared not blurt out what I was thinking, since I did not think my captors would find it too amusing, and there would be repercussions. Not pleasant ones, either.

Nonetheless, I tried to stay alert to my surroundings and not let my judgment be clouded. They were telling so many contradictory stories, and they would change often. I realized that these criminals did not have a clue as to what they were doing and were improvising as they went along. They may have just been lying to me to keep me off balance. In any case, their behavior made it exasperating at times to try to decipher what their plans were.

Keeping my mind clear also allowed me to play mental games with my captors. It was the only amusement I had, and it made for a good laugh, telling them things to throw them off and see how they would react. They never caught on that I was just telling them things so they would feel good when, in fact, I wanted the opposite. They were not intelligent, which made my games more fun but also more dangerous.

One of their favorite games was telling the different plans they had for my release. I always knew they were just stories to pacify me and so that I would not put up resistance and give them what they wanted. I always played along with them even though I knew they were lying. With each new story I would act eager and try making them believe they were duping me. I would ask them questions and appear gullible.

Another favorite pastime of my captors was to

tell me they worked for different government agencies; FBI and CIA were their favorites. I would just listen and make them think I believed them. When in reality all I wanted to do was laugh.

Until the end, I did not allow my guard to fall or my thoughts to stray. I was always alert because I knew that, at any moment, an opportunity could arise to help me escape the warehouse. Unfortunately, that opportunity never arose.

My mind and spirit helped me survive those dark days in that warehouse. I use these same qualities now that I am a free man, free from those chains. I knew what needed to be done from the moment I woke up in the ICU of Jackson Memorial Hospital.

To cleanse my mind, and with the encouragement of my friend Gene Rosen, I sat down to write my story during the first week of January 1995. I spent two weeks and wrote more than two hundred pages of detailed notes on what had occurred in the warehouse. It was a purging that was very important.

While I was in the hospital, I began to plan. Even though I was groggy from the drugs, I would call credit card companies and banks to see what was left. There was not much. I needed clarity and the peace to think of what would become of my life. My options were completely open. I had no home, no business, and basically no material possessions to speak of. In fact, the clothes that I had walked out of the hospital with were borrowed. But in my mind I had always been a fighter, and I knew that this was just another challenge I had to face.

I had always been a rock, a pillar of strength for others and myself. These events, no matter how tragic or traumatic, were not going to change that.

I did suffer from nightmares in the beginning, and I would wake up sweating, shaking or yanking my left arm to see if I was attached to the chains. In most of the nightmares, I was still in the warehouse, getting ready for another helping of torture or something similar. In time, they became less frequent, and eventually they went away altogether. It has now been years since I have had one. Time has healed that, as well.

While I was in New York, I could not take a mental vacation. There were important issues to confront. Where would we live? What would I do? The most important task was to bring the criminals to justice. In that regard, I was fortunate, as Ed DuBois, a private investigator became my closest ally. At first, Ed thought my story was wild, but the more he looked into it, he became convinced that I was telling the truth.

My role the investigation was solely to provide Ed with information. Ed handled everything masterfully and at great risk to himself and his family. I could only wait and see what new details he would uncover.

An attorney friend of mine, Gene Rosen, handled the process of regaining my house and any other assets that had not already disappeared. He would not only do the necessary investigation but also file the documents to regain possession. There was not much to get back, but whatever remained, Gene got for me.

In that respect, I was very fortunate, as the right people had appeared at the right time in my life to help me. Most days I sat by the window at my sister's house, looking out for any suspicion vehicle or movement. Remember, this was the Big Apple. Suspicious was the norm there. I tried not to think about the past or the future and just tried being in the moment. The immediate past was a horror story, and the immediate future was unknown. So why go there?

I finally decided that I could not live with that paranoia, and left the United States to get my health and mind back in proper working order.

While I was in Colombia, my captivity almost seemed as if it had been a bad dream. The calls from Gene and Ed reminded me that it had been real, but, for moments, I could escape that reality.

I spent quality time with my young children when they got home from school, either playing games or helping them do their homework. It had been just over two months ago that I had a tearful conversation with my son from the warehouse with a gun to my head, that I was sure would be my last. Now, I found myself in moments of pure joy simply by being with him.

During the day, when my children were in school, I would sit by the window and look at the gardens for hours in childish amazement, at the beauty of the flowers, the trees and all the vibrant colors, thinking how fortunate I was that I could see again and hear the sweet melodies of the birds singing. This was something that, not so long ago, I had thought would never be.

Slowly but surely I started attending to those things that needed to be done. My thoughts strayed less and less to the events in the warehouse. Slowly I began to have a routine again, a life and a measure of peace. That would not last, but gave me enough time for my mind to recuperate, and my batteries to recharge to fight on.

I rarely talked to anyone about what I had endured. Who could understand? Words could never describe it. I did not even talk to my wife about it. I felt that it was useless trying to tell anyone what one feels in such extreme circumstances. There are some things there are no words for, and this was one of them.

I always knew that my mental state depended on me. No one, no matter how much they cared or wanted to help me, could do so. I was the captain of my own ship, and whether I sailed smoothly or hit rocks would be my own doing. It would be my responsibility to straighten the ship's course once again.

I believe that, for the most part, I have been able to get my ship to sail on smooth waters. I'm ever vigilant for any rocks that may ground me. My mind is at peace, and, as with any muscle, those events of long ago have strengthened it. I move on in the journey of life, learning its lessons, looking to help others who have strayed from their course and run into rocks.

The mind is fragile and it can be our greatest ally or enemy. I recognized that both during the days I was in the warehouse and afterwards. Nurturing it with positive thoughts and not letting it stray too far from the situation at hand helped me to survive and be triumphant afterwards. Ever since I was a child I knew that victory or defeat was ultimately up to me no matter what the situation was. This episode in my life was no different.

CHAPTER 7

The Soul

"Our soul, our true self, is the most mysterious, essential, and magical dimension of our being. In fact, it is not a separate reality, as traditional Western thought views it, but the cohesive force that unites our body, heart, and mind. It is not a ghost trapped somehow in the physical machinery of our body but the very essence of our being"—Gabrielle Roth

I was reborn the day I walked out of the New York hospital. Any innocence I may have had was now gone. The way I saw the world and its inhabitants had forever changed. This was a new beginning, and I was blessed to have another chance. I was thankful despite all that had happened to me, because I knew that my survival was miraculous.

During my stay in Hotel Hell, I never felt alone or abandoned by Source Energy, All That Is, or God, whatever term you prefer for the omnipotent and omnipresent power. As I mentioned before, I was not a religious person, but I have always been a person of deep faith. During those days, I felt that someone/something was looking out for me and guiding me in both heart and mind.

I remained steadfast throughout the thirty days, and my faith never faltered. No matter what humiliation or torture I was subjected to. Never did I have ridiculous thoughts go through my mind that I was being punished for something I had done. Although I do believe that what you put out is what you receive, I never felt that I had purposely hurt or done harm to anyone.

In what I was sure would be my final hours, I felt a comforting peace even though I knew that my time was short. I felt neither fearful nor alone. Need

I say more than is evident by my miraculous survival? I do not recall the events after I was drugged at the warehouse. I was unconscious. In fact, when the paramedics transported me to the hospital, I was in a coma.

How I was able to get out of the burning car remains a mystery. To me, it's clear that my guardian angels or spiritual guides were there to save me. There is no other explanation or answer. It was supernatural and beyond the understanding of most humans. Even more incredible was the fact that I survived being run over by a car twice with no long-term consequences.

In my sister's case her time had come, her journey was complete. I never blamed God for her passing or even questioned the reason she had moved on. My mission was not complete. I either had more to do in this life or had to help others do more in theirs. I have learned that there is no such thing as untimely death. We move on when what we came here to do is complete, no sooner, no later.

My experience has also benefited me in that it has given me a greater understanding of life, and I have been able to develop a sense of inner peace. I live for the now and look for joy in everything I do. I have learned to forgive my tormentors and anyone else who commits any transgressions against me.

This experience opened new doors in spirituality for me. It was the beginning of a search and learning process about the spirit realm that continues today. It is a journey to learn who I truly am and how our thoughts and actions determine our reality. It has been an enriching experience, and I'm always discovering new doorways and paths that add to who I am.

I'm convinced that my deep faith guided me and helped me survive those dark days in the warehouse, and they guide me today to be a better human being to my fellow man.

CHAPTER 8

Totality

"Humankind has not woven the web of life; we are but one thread in it. What we do to the web, we do to ourselves. All things are bound together. All things connect"—Chief Seattle

It has been a long and winding road to get to where I find myself today. Upon gaining my freedom, I promised to leave those events in the past and not look back. I reasoned that dwelling on those events could not benefit me in any way, but doing so could cause me harm and not allow me to move forward on my life's journey. There have been other difficult moments since those events, but with the inner strength I have found, they are merely bumps on the road. I've come to realize that what I get out of life is up to me. The perspective I choose to look at events and individuals ultimately determines the way I see life itself and how I live it. I have chosen to look at the beauty and wonder of everything that surrounds me and live in joy. The choice of how you live and see your life is up to you.

I have also chosen to forgive the individuals who perpetrated those heinous acts against me. I choose not to hate and not to be angry. It is part of my healing, and it gives me the freedom to move on without carrying the baggage of the past.

What I want the reader to take away from this book is that anyone and everyone can overcome anything. Doing so takes the right mental attitude and fortitude, along with having the faith and spirit to triumph.

The message is simple: Stop feeling sorry for yourself. Count your blessings, not your sorrows. The power to change things lies within each of us. Recognize it and grasp it.

Look within yourself, not outside.

We are spiritual beings having a human experience.

I do not want to convince anyone that I'm different or possess any special qualities that helped me not only survive but thrive. We as humans all possess these qualities, whether or not we recognize them. My intent is to make you who are reading these pages aware that you also possess the inner strength and spirit to overcome any difficult or traumatic situation. The answer lies within you.

Live life in simple terms:

We are sum of our life experiences.

Live for today, and enjoy each experience to the fullest.

Count your blessings every day.

If, upon the journey of life, you run into obstacles or unpleasant experiences, always remember that you have the inner strength and wisdom to overcome and be victorious in any situation.

Don't take those around you for granted: family, loved ones and friends. Tell them how much you appreciate them every day. Give them a hug. Hugs are the medicine of the soul.

Smile and laugh. . . .

In the end, it's not the game but how you played it that matters.

Remember, the sun comes out after each rain and warms our hearts.

Show appreciation and be thankful each day for all the blessings you receive.

I'm the sum of my life experiences, countless sorrows and joys. They have all taught me and helped me grow.

I feel blessed to have been able to share this book with you, knowing that someone out there took this message to heart and found the inner strength to move forward with his or her life.

So, as I continue on my life's journey, it is my hope that my love, words, and guiding and helping hand will help another. But remember that your life is what you make of it, and it is always ultimately up to you.

Marc Schiller

Namaste
Love and Peace Surround You Always, and
May Your Spirit Soar

ABOUT THE AUTHOR

Marc Schiller was born in Buenos Aires, Argentina, immigrating to Brooklyn, New York, with his parents when he was seven years old. An early entrepreneur, he started several small businesses by the age of nine. He attended high school in Brooklyn, participating in sports and as a member of the school's track team.

Marc received a bachelor's degree in accounting from the University of Wisconsin-Milwaukee and an MBA from Benedictine University. Marc has had a long and diversified career as both a professional and an entrepreneur. His professional career has spanned the US and the world. On an entrepreneurial level, Marc Schiller has launched several successful businesses, including two accounting practices both in Miami and Houston, a delicatessen in Miami, and an options and stock trading company.

Marc is also the author of *Pain and Gain: The Untold True Story*, published in January 2013.

Made in the USA
San Bernardino, CA
15 February 2014